make it in
Minutes

Memory Jewelry

make it in
Minutes

Memory Jewelry

LIZ EATON

A Division of Sterling Publishing Co., Inc.
New York / London

Book Editor
Lecia Monsen

Copy Editors
Lisa Anderson
Karmen Quinney
Catherine Risling

Book Designer
Kehoe + Kehoe Design
Associates, Inc.

Photographer
Zachary Williams
Williams Visual

Stylist
Brittany Aardema

*Other Books
in This Series:*

Make It in Minutes:
Greeting Cards

Make It in Minutes:
Mini-Books

Make It in Minutes:
Mini-Boxes

Make It in Minutes:
Beaded Jewelry

Make It in Minutes:
Party Favors
& Hostess Gifts

Make It in Minutes:
Felt Accessories

Make It in Minutes:
Faux Floral Arrangements

Make It in Minutes:
Quick & Clever
Gift Wraps

A Red Lips 4 Courage Communications, Inc., book
www.redlips4courage.com
Eileen Cannon Paulin
President
Catherine Risling
Director of Editorial

Library of Congress Cataloging-in-Publication Data

Make it in minutes : memory jewelry / [Lecia Monsen, editor]. -- 1st ed.
    p. cm.
Includes index.
ISBN-13: 978-1-60059-227-0 (alk. paper)
ISBN-10: 1-60059-227-9 (alk. paper)
1. Jewelry making. I. Monsen, Lecia. II. Title: Memory jewelry.
TT212.M65 2008
745.594'2--dc22

                                        2007030160

10 9 8 7 6 5 4 3 2 1

First Edition

Published by Lark Books, A Division of
Sterling Publishing Co., Inc.
387 Park Avenue South, New York, NY 10016

Text © 2008, Liz Eaton
Photography © 2008, Red Lips 4 Courage Communications, Inc.
Illustrations © 2008, Red Lips 4 Courage Communications, Inc.

Distributed in Canada by Sterling Publishing,
c/o Canadian Manda Group, 165 Dufferin Street
Toronto, Ontario, Canada M6K 3H6

Distributed in the United Kingdom by GMC Distribution Services,
Castle Place, 166 High Street, Lewes, East Sussex, England BN7 1XU

Distributed in Australia by Capricorn Link (Australia) Pty Ltd.,
P.O. Box 704, Windsor, NSW 2756 Australia

If you have questions or comments about this book, please contact:
Lark Books
67 Broadway
Asheville, NC 28801
(828) 253-0467

Manufactured in China

ISBN 13: 978-1-60059-227-0

For information about custom editions, special sales, premium and corporate
purchases, please contact Sterling Special Sales Department at (800) 805-5489
or specialsales@sterlingpub.com.

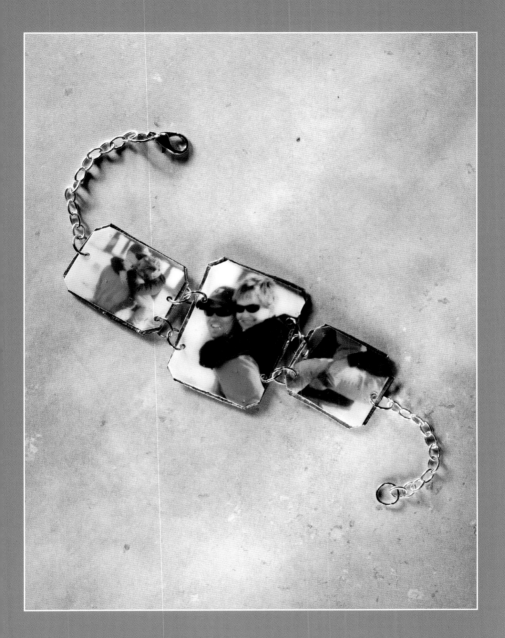

"If you want to keep your memories,
you first have to live them."
—Bob Dylan

Contents

Introduction

All types of jewelry have been around for thousands of years and have adorned the bodies of men, women, and children. Wearing jewelry was a visible way of demonstrating one's class, wealth, success, and identity. In this book I've added an additional dimension using favorite memories.

Memories remind us of who we are and what we've done, and accompany us to where we're going. These experiences may happen on family vacations, when traveling the world, or maybe just in the kitchen with your mom. I'll show you how to turn the recollections in your head into tangible jewelry pieces to be seen and cherished. The best part of this whole process is that each piece in this book can be done within an hour, so start reminiscing and explore what inspired me in the following pages.

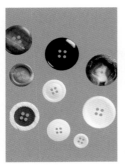

CHAPTER 1

In this chapter you will explore the main elements that will help you incorporate a special memory into a piece of jewelry in just minutes. Jewelry making is a craft like any other and therefore has supplies and tools that need explanation and techniques you will need to be aware of while working on your projects.

The supplies for memory jewelry making are endless and only stop where your imagination does, but I've listed and explained the main ingredients for the process. I recommend that before you get started creating you read through this chapter carefully to educate yourself on the many different materials, tools, and techniques that will help you succeed.

Getting Started

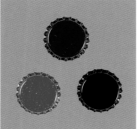
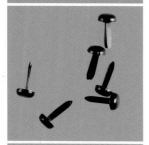
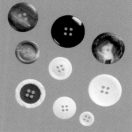

Embellishments

Beads

Beads are made in all parts of the world in every shape and color and in many different materials such as bone, wood, clay, glass, shell, and metal. Many years ago beads were used as money for trading and bartering. Many of the projects in this book use these types of beads from Africa.

Bottle caps

Bottle caps are made in a variety of colors but are generally manufactured in one size and can be found in most craft stores in bulk amounts. They are used as embellishments in scrapbooking and as jewelry elements.

Brads

Brads come in many different colors, shapes, and styles. They vary in size ranging from $\frac{1}{16}$" to $\frac{1}{2}$". All brads have prongs that are threaded through a small hole in the project that are then opened and flattened to secure them in place.

Buttons

Buttons come in many different sizes, colors, and finishes. They add a dimensional element to any project. Clear buttons can perform the same duty as glass in a frame by protecting an image that is adhered to the back of the button.

Charms

Charms are made out of metal, glass, plastic, or wood. They come in many different images and icons. Pretty much anything you are looking for can be found in a charm: for instance, a butterfly or bicycle.

Chipboard

Chipboard is a smooth, pressed cardboard made out of paper stock and ranges in thickness from $\frac{1}{32}$" and up. All the projects in this book use the thinnest chipboard. Some chipboard is acid-free but most are not. If you need acid-free, make sure you ask for it specifically at a craft store.

Cord
Cord is thick string wrapped in different colors of leather or vinyl. It is flexible and can be used for stringing beads and as a chain for jewelry projects.

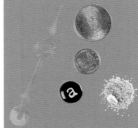

Found objects
Found objects are anything collected from antique stores, garage sales, or vintage shops. They are simply items that don't have a home until you give them one in your craft projects.

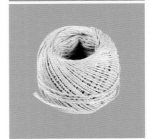

Hemp
Hemp is a natural fiber extracted from the stem of a plant. It is used to make rope that comes in various sizes. For jewelry purposes, 18-gauge hemp is used for stringing beads and charms.

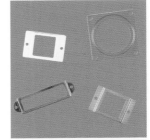

Label holders
Label holders started out being used in offices to label drawers, but they have more recently been used in scrapbooking to add texture and depth to projects as well as in home décor. A label holder can also be hung from a jump ring attached to a chain and worn as a charm.

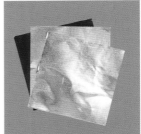

Metal sheets
Metal sheets come in a variety of sizes and thicknesses and are made from different types of metal such as copper, nickel, silver, or even gold. For most craft projects, 32-gauge metal is best to use because it is easy to manipulate and cut with regular scissors.

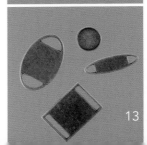

Ribbon slides
Ribbon slides are similar to charms and are usually made of metal. They have a slit on two edges through which ribbon or other thin, pliable material, like hemp or leather, can be threaded to hold the slide and to show the design of the metal face.

Tools

Acrylic paint

Bone folder

Chain-nose pliers

Circle punch

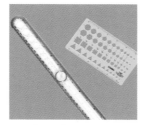

Circle rulers

Craft glue

Craft knife

Dimensional adhesive

Embossing ink

Embossing powder

Embossing tools

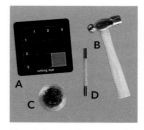

Eyelet setting tools
A Setting mat   C Eyelets
B Craft hammer   D Eyelet setter

Flat-head screwdriver

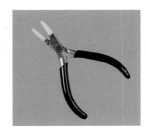

Flat-nose pliers

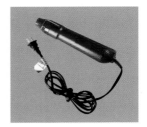

Heat tool

Hole punch

Nail polish remover

Piercing tool

Power drill and metal cutting bits

Round-nose pliers

Rubber stamps

Soldering tools

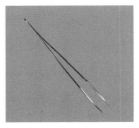

Tweezers

Wire cutters

Findings

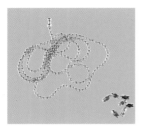

Ball chain and clasp

Barrettes

Clasps

Cord ends

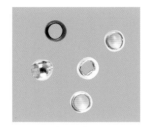

Crimp beads

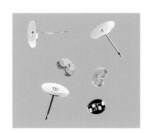

Earring posts

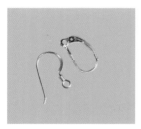

Earring wires

Head pins

Jump rings

Medium cable chain

Pin backs

Tie tacs

Techniques

■ Crimping

Crimping is the best method to begin or finish the end of a strung piece of jewelry like a bracelet, necklace, or anklet that needs a loop on one end for the clasp. You will need wire, a crimping bead, and a pair of chain-nose pliers. Thread the wire through the crimping bead, then make a small loop about ½" and thread wire end back through the bead (Fig. 1). Flatten the crimp with the pliers until the bead holds the wire in place (Fig. 2). Tug on the wire to make sure it does not slip out of the bead.

■ Wrapping Head Pins

Sometimes a jump ring won't work when connecting an element to a piece of jewelry. In cases like this, a head pin is a useful option. You will need a 3" head pin, chain-nose pliers, round-nose pliers, wire cutters, a button with a shank, and a piece of jewelry. Thread the head pin through the button shank (Fig. 3). Form a loop in the head pin above the shank using the round-nose pliers (Fig. 4). Holding the button with chain-nose pliers, thread wire end back through shank (Fig. 5). Attach the button to the jewelry piece by repeating the process. Trim any excess wire with wire cutters.

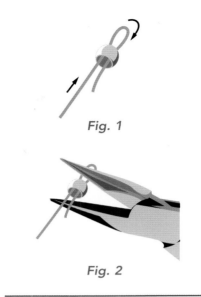

Fig. 1

Fig. 2

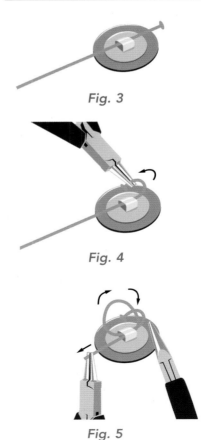

Fig. 3

Fig. 4

Fig. 5

17

Fig. 1

Fig. 2

Fig. 3

Fig. 4

Fig. 5

■ *Metal Embossing*

Using rubber stamps and a permanent inkpad, stamp an image onto a piece of 32-gauge sheet metal or draw one freehand using a stylus (Fig. 1). Place sheet metal on a ⅛" foam pad and firmly trace the stamped image with the stylus (Fig. 2). Turn the sheet over and emboss the inside of the image (Fig. 3). Once you are satisfied with the image, use acrylic paint and a cloth or sponge to highlight the image, creating a patina that enhances the dimensional feel (Fig. 4). When the acrylic paint is dry, use steel wool to remove some of the ink from the stamped image. When choosing an image to emboss, a simple one usually works best with the rubber stamp (Fig. 5). *Note:* To create more definition, flip the piece over and emboss reverse side for added interest.

■ *Sanding*

Using this technique softens the edges of paper and photos for an aged or distressed look. Sandpaper comes in many different grit sizes, but when working with paper or photos, 150-grit is best. An emery board is very useful for working in small areas. Use light to medium pressure with the sandpaper on the surface to be distressed until the desired look is achieved.

Fig. 6

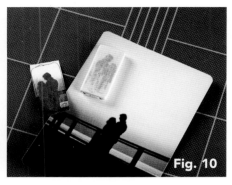

Fig. 10

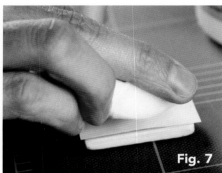

Fig. 7

■ *Photo Transferring*

This technique can be done on most any type of fairly smooth surface such as paper, fabric, wood, or beads. Place a photocopy facedown on the project's surface (Fig. 6). Apply a generous amount of nail polish remover on the back of the paper using a cosmetic sponge (Fig. 7). Firmly rub the back of the photocopy with a bone folder (Fig. 8). Slowly lift the corner to see if the transfer is complete (Fig. 9). If it's not, simply lay the paper back down and continue to rub until the image is completely transferred (Fig. 10). *Note:* If you're having trouble getting an image to transfer, try using a colorless xylene blending pen instead of nail polish remover. When using a blending pen, be sure to work in a well-ventilated area and use a light application. Apply the solvent until you can see the photocopied image through the paper. Rub the back of the photocopy with the bone folder as stated above. Once the image is transferred and dry, apply a protective sealant like decoupage glue to protect it from wear and tear. Also be sure to use photocopies because an ink jet or laser print will not transfer well.

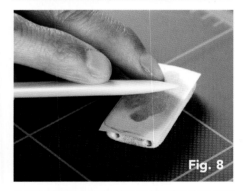

Fig. 8

Fig. 9

■ Soldering

Soldering joins two pieces of metal by melting them together. It is roughly similar to welding and can be used on most any surface, such as glass, buttons, or chipboard, as long as the surface has copper foil tape attached to it. If the element is already made of metal, like a charm or jump ring, the soldering iron will melt it without requiring copper foil tape. Plug the soldering iron in and allow it to heat up. Tape around the outside edges of the project using copper foil tape (Fig. 1) and then burnish with a bone folder to make sure all the wrinkles are smoothed out and the tape is tightly secured to the project (Fig. 2). Paint flux onto all copper foil surface with a cotton swab or cosmetic sponge (Fig. 3). Heat all edges covering the copper foil with soldering iron (Fig. 4). Add a jump ring to the top of the piece, if desired, by holding jump ring in place with chain-nose pliers and using the soldering iron to connect the jump ring to the soldered edge. Let project cool and then wipe off excess flux and clean with a wet cloth. *Note:* The iron will get very hot and can burn you and anything else flammable it may touch. Keep it and the other soldering tools out of reach of children.

time-saving tip

Organizing Jump Rings

Jump rings are probably the most often-used element when it comes to making any jewelry piece. It's very handy to keep a variety of jump rings on hand. I like to organize mine in a small divided plastic container that has a lid.

■ Drilling

In the jewelry-making process, drilling through different materials is one of the best and easiest ways to attach multiple items together. There are a few different types of drills, from hand-cranked to cordless power drills. You will need a power drill, metal bits in various sizes, a scrap piece of wood, and a C clamp with plastic ends so you won't harm the surface of the project. Choose the appropriate size of metal bit for your project and tighten it in your drill following the manufacturer's instructions. Clamp the material to be drilled to the piece of scrap wood using the C clamp. Position the drill, and using firm pressure, drill into the piece until you hit the scrap wood.

■ Using Jump Rings

Using two pairs of pliers, such as a flat-nose and chain-nose, grasp jump ring on either side of the opening. Gently pull one side of the ring toward you and the other away from you until it's open far enough to use in the project (Fig. 5). To close, do the opposite, pulling inward until the ring ends meet. This same technique can also be used with fishhook earring wires.

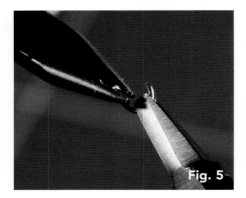

Fig. 5

Tying Knots

Fig. 6

■ Square knot: Hold ends of stringing material in each hand. Cross left end over right end and wrap under as if you were tying your shoes. Wrap right end over left end, then under left end and pull both ends to tighten (Fig. 6).

Fig. 7

■ Single knot or overhand knot: Hold the stringing material and form a loop, then thread one end through the loop and pull tight (Fig. 7).

Fig. 8

■ Double knot: Tie a single knot, but before pulling it tight, thread the end through the loop one more time and tighten (Fig. 8).

CHAPTER 2

It's time to put a twist on the everyday bracelet and customize one for a special occasion you want to remember forever. What better way to show off photos of a favorite vacation or loved ones than a bracelet for others to see and for you to wear every day? The keepsakes in this chapter cover occasions that range from traveling the world to celebrating an anniversary to spending time with family and friends. When thinking about making a keepsake bracelet, consider not only how photos can be transformed into jewelry but also modifying some of the components that are used to make a piece. On the following pages you will find many ways to customize the perfect one-of-a kind memory bracelet.

24

Amsterdam

Amsterdam was my first experience traveling to Europe. I immediately fell in love with the architecture, street signs, and historic feel of the city. I transferred some of the sign images onto two beads and added the date and location of my trip to the third bead. This is a simple way of recording impressions of a special event or trip.

Materials

- Beads: ½" African trading (2); 1½" bamboo (3)
- Bone folder
- Color-copied images (2)
- Cosmetic sponge
- Decoupage glue
- Hemp: natural (10")
- Jump ring: 7mm silver
- Nail polish remover
- Rub-ons: alphabet, numbers
- Toggle clasp: medium silver

Instructions

1. Transfer photocopied images onto two bamboo beads with nail polish remover and bone folder.

2. Spell name and date on remaining bamboo bead using rub-ons.

3. Sponge decoupage glue over image transfers and rub-ons with cosmetic sponge; let dry.

4. Separate hemp into two strands and string bamboo and African beads together as shown in project photo, tying a square knot between each bead.

5. Connect jump ring to toggle clasp on hemp ends with another square knot.

time-saving tip

Photo Transfer Prints

When printing photos for projects, make several copies of each to have on hand for other projects.

Baby Sam

I wanted my nephew to be able to wear this bracelet home from the hospital so I made it very small. Once he is old enough to put things in his mouth, this will probably be better as a keepsake for his mother to enjoy. It would be easy to convert it into a bracelet by adding more cable chain so that additional charms to commemorate new milestones as he grows can be attached.

Materials

- Chain: silver medium cable (4½")
- Charms: silver, baby-themed, square frame (5)
- Craft glue
- Jump rings: silver 4mm (6), 7mm (5)
- Lobster claw clasp: 12mm silver
- Photos (2)
- Pliers: chain-nose, flat-nose
- Scissors
- Stickers: ½" square clear pebble (2)

Instructions

1. Trim photos to fit front and back of square charm and adhere with craft glue; let dry. Cover photos with pebble stickers.

2. Attach clasp to one end of chain length using 4mm jump ring and both pliers. Add 7mm jump ring to the other end.

3. Attach charms to chain with remaining jump rings using both pliers.

time-saving tip

Custom-Length Chains

Most chains can be purchased by the inch, making it easy to customize a bracelet or necklace for a specific person. The only tools needed to cut bulk chain are wire cutters.

Dirt Bike Dreams

Bracelets aren't just for women. The men in our lives might like to wear jewelry too, at least the man in mine does. This bracelet honors his love for dirt biking and being outdoors. This idea can be easily modified for a feminine recipient by using two coordinating ribbons in different widths and a charm to highlight the photo.

Materials

- Adhesives: craft glue, dimensional adhesive
- Charm: silver gear
- Jump ring: 7mm silver
- Leather bracelet: 9" brown
- Photo
- Pliers: chain-nose, flat-nose
- Ribbon slide: 1¼" silver
- Scissors

Instructions

1. Trim photo to fit center of ribbon slide and adhere with craft glue; let dry.

2. Cover photo with dimensional adhesive; let dry.

3. Thread ribbon slide onto leather bracelet. Attach charm to slide with jump ring using both pliers.

time-saving tip

Ribbon Slide Photo Frames

You can customize any ribbon slide to fit your memory jewelry. The flat area in the center of a slide is a perfect spot for a photo. The slide used in this project had words on it that didn't apply to what I wanted to capture in the memory, so I covered it with a photo and dimensional adhesive.

Families

Family is very important to both my mother and me so I made this bracelet for her. She has six grown kids who all have families of their own. This piece shows all six families she has helped nurture. The bracelet is a great way to show a sequence of events or milestones by using related photos to tell a story.

Materials

- Adhesives: craft glue, dimensional adhesive
- Charm frame bracelet: 8" silver with fold-over clasp
- Photos: $\frac{3}{4}$" x $\frac{5}{8}$" (6)
- Scissors

Instructions

1. Trim photos to fit frames. Adhere photo to each frame with craft glue; let dry.

2. Cover each photo with dimensional adhesive; let dry.

time-saving tip

Finding Photos

Showing off your memories to their best advantage starts with having plenty of good-quality photos. Before any event, think about the types of things you will want to feature. Having a game plan before you are caught in the heat of the moment will help you take better pictures. For those occasions that arrived unexpectedly, make sure the subjects are close together with plenty of space around the group so that you don't accidentally crop off something important when you put your project together.

Flea Market Finds

I love taking purely inspirational trips to places like antique malls, garage sales, and especially flea markets. This project showcases photos of my first experience at a flea market. I was instantly hooked on all the wonderful things I found. I used label holders from my scrapbooking stash as frames. The charms are also from my crafting supplies and are readily available at most craft stores. I used them because they just seemed to support the feeling I had when I was visiting the flea market.

Materials

- Adhesives: craft glue, dimensional adhesive
- C clamp
- Charm bracelet: 8" silver with toggle clasp
- Charms (4)
- Jump rings: 7mm silver (7)
- Label holders: $\frac{1}{2}$"x 1$\frac{3}{4}$" brass; $\frac{3}{4}$"x 1$\frac{1}{4}$" silver (2)
- Patterned paper scraps: coordinating colors
- Photos (3)
- Pliers: chain-nose, flat-nose
- Power drill and .051mm metal bit
- Scissors

Instructions

1. Trim photos to fit label holders and adhere inside with craft glue; let dry.

2. Cut patterned paper to fit back of each label holder. Glue in place and cover with dimensional adhesive; let dry.

3. Drill holes in charms using C clamp, power drill, and bit.

4. Attach charms and label holders to bracelet with jump rings using both pliers.

time-saving tip

Getting a Professional Finish
Good craftsmanship really makes a piece of jewelry stand out. Patterned paper is a quick and easy way to cover the back of a photo or project to give a handmade piece a more finished look.

Fourth Anniversary

My husband and I recently celebrated our fourth wedding anniversary. I made this bracelet in honor of our love for each other.

Materials

- Acrylic paint: black
- Adhesives: craft glue, dimensional adhesive
- Chain: silver medium cable (4")
- Embossing stylus
- Hole punch: ¹⁄₁₆"
- Inkpad: permanent black
- Jump rings: 7mm gold (10)
- Lobster claw clasp: 12mm gold
- Metal sheet: 32-gauge copper (4" square)
- Photos (3)
- Pliers: chain-nose, flat-nose
- Rubber stamps
- Ruler
- Scissors
- Wire cutters

Instructions

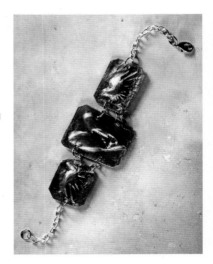

1. Emboss designs on copper sheet using rubber stamps, inkpad, embossing stylus, and acrylic paint.

2. Trim embossed designs with scissors, leaving additional ¼" around outside. Fold sides over ⅛" using chain-nose pliers, creating a straight edge.

3. Trim photos to fit back of each embossed copper piece and adhere with craft glue. Cover photos with dimensional adhesive; let dry.

4. Punch holes on sides of each piece as shown in project photo using hole punch.

5. Attach all pieces together using jump rings and both pliers. Cut two 2" lengths of chain using wire cutters and attach to either end of linked copper pieces. Attach clasp and jump ring to each end of bracelet.

Measure Love

My husband and I have known each other since we were 13 years old. The old ruler paper I used suggests the early days of school, which is where we started, and the current photos of us show where we are today. Adapt this idea to showcase photos of your child from each of his or her grade school years.

Materials

- Bracelet kit: brass links with lobster claw clasp
- Charms: ¾" brass circles with links (6)
- Circle ruler
- Craft glue
- Craft knife
- Patterned paper scraps: measuring tape
- Photos (3)
- Pliers: chain-nose, flat-nose
- Stickers: ¾" round clear pebble (6)

Instructions

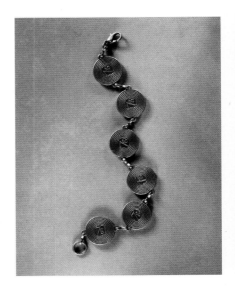

1. Trim patterned paper and photos to fit circle charms using craft knife and circle ruler. Adhere to charms with craft glue; let dry.

2. Place pebble stickers over each embellished charm.

3. Connect all charms together using links and both pliers. Crimp link centers by squeezing with chain-nose pliers, making sure to keep one charm on either side of crimp. Add clasp to bracelet ends in same manner.

time-saving tip

Working with Jewelry Kits

Pre-assembled jewelry kits are a quick and simple way to make a perfect keepsake by adding your own memorable touches. It looks like you invested a lot of time but each piece can usually be completed in less than an hour.

Three Sisters

My oldest sister has three beautiful girls who are growing up way too fast. I thought this would be a wonderful gift to help her remember that no matter how old her kids are getting, they will always be mommy's little girls.

Materials

- Adhesives: craft glue, dimensional adhesive
- C clamp
- Chain: silver medium cable (2")
- Circle ruler
- Craft knife
- Jump rings: silver 4mm (2), 7mm (8)
- Photos (3)
- Pliers: chain-nose, flat-nose
- Power drill and .051mm metal bit
- Stickers: ½" black-and-white number; ½" silver stars (3)
- Toggle clasp: 2" silver
- Typewriter keys: ½" copper (7)

Instructions

1. Cut three ½" circles from photos using circle ruler and craft knife. Adhere trimmed photos inside of typewriter keys with craft glue; let dry.

2. Place stickers inside remaining keys as desired. Fill all keys with dimensional adhesive; let dry.

3. Drill holes on both sides of each key using C clamp, power drill, and bit.

4. Connect keys together with 7mm jump rings using both pliers.

5. Add chain to one side of bracelet with jump ring as shown in project photo. Connect toggle clasp to ends with 4mm jump rings.

CHAPTER 3

Everyone, children or adults, men or women, can wear a necklace. Just as individuals in the military wear dog tags to let others know who they are, necklaces can communicate a great deal about a person. They can honor a loved one, highlight a hobby, show your love for your family, or simply hold memories from your latest vacation. In this chapter you will find many unique ways to use ordinary supplies from around the house. Don't be afraid to jump in and start exploring the many different ways to make a necklace for yourself or as a gift for someone else. With these instructions and tips, it will be a snap to create a necklace in hardly any time at all.

7005 Home

I made this project in honor of the first home my husband and I lived in as a married couple. It shows our house number and the initial of our last name.

Materials

- Ball clasp: silver
- Bottle cap: 1½" silver
- C clamp
- Chain: silver ball (18")
- Charm: mini silver key
- Circle punch: 1"
- Craft glue
- Gaffer tape: numbers

- Heat tool
- Jump rings: 7mm silver (2)
- Patterned paper scraps: coordinating colors
- Pliers: chain-nose, flat-nose
- Power drill and .070mm metal bit
- Rub-ons: alphabets, numbers
- Scissors
- Ultra-thick embossing powder: clear

Instructions

1. Punch circle of patterned paper with circle punch and adhere to inside center of bottle cap using craft glue.

2. Cut out gaffer tape, rub-on numbers, and patterned paper as desired. Apply rub-ons and adhere cutouts to patterned paper background.

3. Fill bottle cap with embossing powder and melt with heat tool; let cool.

4. Drill holes at top and slightly off-center on bottom of bottle cap using C clamp, power drill, and bit. Add key charm to bottom hole with jump ring using both pliers.

5. Add remaining jump ring to top of cap using both pliers. String ball chain through top jump ring and snap clasp onto chain.

time-saving tip

Applying a Clear Coat
Give your project a glossy finish by using clear ultra-thick embossing powder. As long as the heat tool won't ruin the items used in the project, this is an easy way to get a professional look.

Eleven Weeks

When I found out I was expecting my first child, I thought making a necklace or ornament for each week would be a wonderful way to remember my pregnancy, moods, and how I felt waiting for my baby's arrival. This is the first ornament I made.

Materials

- Bone folder
- Cord: black leather (18")
- Cord ends: silver (2)
- Foil tape: silver
- Glass slides: 1" x 3" (2)
- Jump ring: 7mm silver
- Lobster claw clasp: 12mm silver
- Patterned paper scraps: coordinating colors
- Pliers: chain-nose, flat-nose
- Rub-ons: alphabets, images
- Ruler
- Scissors
- Soldering iron and flux
- Stickers: designs, numbers

Instructions

1. Cut two 1" x 3" pieces of patterned paper. Adhere stickers and rub-ons to both pieces as desired.

2. Place embellished paper pieces back to back and insert between glass slides. Seal slides together using foil tape and bone folder. Solder foil edges and jump ring to top of sealed slides.

3. String cord through jump ring on top of soldered charm. Add cord ends and pinch tight with chain-nose pliers. Attach clasp to loops on cord ends using both pliers.

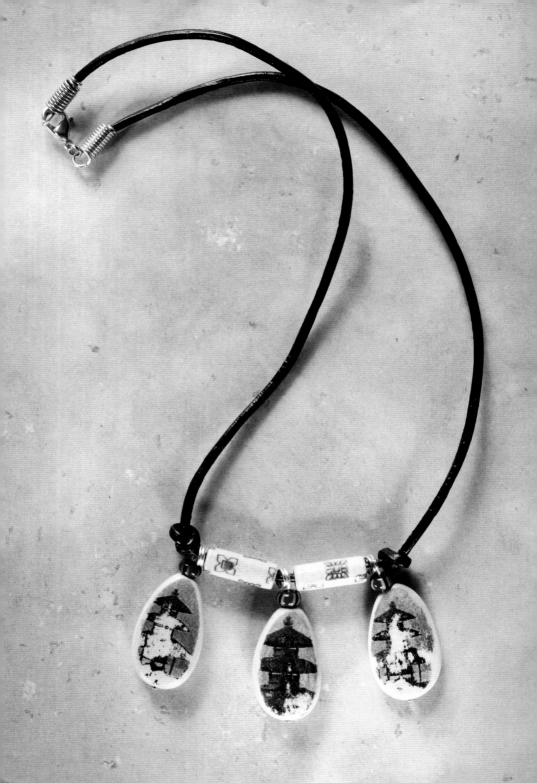

Bali Sanctuaries

When I was in college I was lucky enough to study abroad in Bali, Indonesia. It was a once-in-a-lifetime opportunity that I never want to forget, so I made this necklace to remind me of my time there.

Materials

- Beads: ¼" African trading (3); ¾" flower (2); 1" wood (3)
- Bone folder
- Color-copied images (3)
- Cord: black leather (16")
- Cord ends: ⅜" silver coil
- Cosmetic sponge
- Decoupage glue
- Head pins: 3" silver (2)
- Lobster clasp: 12mm silver
- Nail polish remover
- Pliers: chain-nose, flat-nose, round-nose

Instructions

1. Transfer photocopied images onto wood beads with nail polish remover and bone folder. Paint decoupage glue onto beads with cosmetic sponge; let dry.

2. String one wooden and one African bead on head pin as shown in project photo. Bend top of wire to form ⅛" loop using round-nose pliers. Repeat with remaining beads and head pins.

3. String wired and flower beads onto cord in sequence shown in project photo.

4. Tie single knot on side of outside wire stoppers to hold in place.

5. Add cord ends to cord and pinch closed with flat-nose pliers. Add clasp to cord ends using chain-nose and flat-nose pliers.

time-saving tip

Repeating Images

Repeating images on a piece of jewelry or any art conveys importance and adds weight to the subject. I wanted to emphasize the sense of peace found in these serene sanctuaries so I repeated the image of the Bali temple three times.

Butterfly Girl

I made this necklace for my niece who has a special bond with butterflies. I thought the photo pendant and charms would be a perfect way to remind her of her fascination with these beautiful insects.

Materials

- C clamp
- Charm: butterfly
- Cord: pink (18")
- Cord ends: ¼" silver ring
- Craft glue
- Jump rings: 7mm silver (3)
- Pendant: 1"x 1¾" silver oval with jump ring
- Photos (2)
- Pliers: chain-nose, flat-nose
- Power drill and .051mm metal bit
- S clasp: silver
- Scissors
- Stickers: 1"x 1¾" clear oval pebble (2)
- Tile: ¾" wood letter

Instructions

1. Adhere stickers to photos and trim around edges with scissors. Glue photos to oval pendant; let dry.

2. Drill hole in tile using C clamp, power drill, and bit. Attach jump ring to tile using both pliers.

3. Attach remaining jump rings to charm and pendant and then thread all charms onto cord.

4. Thread cord ends onto cord and pinch shut with flat-nose pliers. Attach clasp to one cord end.

time-saving tip

Highlight a Hobby

This type of keepsake necklace works well to showcase children's hobbies to help them remember what they loved as they get older. Use photos of the child involved in the hobby, a charm that represents a favorite pastime, and a monogram representing the recipient's name.

Military Man

My grandfather died when I was only 10 years old. He served in World War II and I wanted to honor him and the service he gave to our country. I made this with his service photo on the front and his birth and death dates on the back.

Materials

- Adhesives: craft glue, dimensional adhesive
- Ball clasp: silver
- Chain: silver ball (16")
- Chipboard
- Hinged frame: 1½" square silver
- Paper trimmer

- Patterned paper scraps: coordinating colors
- Photo
- Rub-ons: numbers
- Ruler
- Scissors
- Studs: ½" silver stars (3)
- Tweezers

Instructions

1. Cut three 1½" squares of chipboard and two 1½" squares of patterned paper using paper trimmer.

2. Layer and glue all three chipboard squares together with craft glue. Cover front and back of chipboard square with patterned paper using craft glue; let dry.

3. Trim photo to 1½" square and adhere to one side of paper-covered chipboard.

4. Following manufacturer's instructions, open frame in upper right hand corner and place embellished chipboard inside; close frame.

5. Add date to patterned paper side of framed square using rub-on numbers.

6. Cover photo with dimensional adhesive and press stars onto photo as desired with tweezers; let dry.

7. Turn frame over and cover backside with dimensional adhesive; let dry.

8. Thread chain through loop in top of frame and snap clasp onto chain ends.

Outdoor Memories

My husband and I love to spend time outdoors. I made this necklace to hold memories from one of the first camping trips we took together. I only had a few photos, just enough to remind me of this special outdoor experience. The bottle contains stickers and charms related to travel.

Materials

- Ball clasp: silver
- Chain: silver ball (18")
- Charms: $\frac{7}{8}$" silver frames (2)
- Dimensional adhesive
- Glass bottle with cork: 1" x 1$\frac{1}{2}$"
- Jump rings: 7mm silver (3)
- Memorabilia
- Photos (2)
- Pliers: chain-nose, flat-nose
- Scissors
- Tweezers

Instructions

1. Trim memorabilia with scissors and place in bottle using tweezers.

2. Trim photos to fit and place inside charms. Cover photos with dimensional adhesive; let dry.

3. Attach one jump ring to each charm using both pliers. Link charms and bottle together with remaining jump ring.

4. String chain through jump ring and connect clasp to chain.

time-saving tip

Memories Under Glass

Glass bottles are a great way to display small keepsakes in your jewelry pieces that otherwise would get lost. Some of the items that store well are sand, rocks, twigs, seashells, and confetti. These items can be added with tweezers or a funnel to keep your work surface from getting messy.

Queen Mother

I made this to honor my mother. She is the matriarch of our family, having raised six children. Inside the box is an image of her and some handmade charms.

Materials

- Acrylic paint: red
- Adhesives: craft glue, dimensional adhesive
- Ball clasp: silver
- Brad: 1/8" red
- C clamp
- Chain: silver ball (16")
- Charms: 1/2" flower, heart
- Cosmetic sponge
- Jump rings: 7mm silver (2)
- Metal-stamped crown
- Mini playing card: 1 1/2"
- Photo
- Pliers: chain-nose, flat-nose
- Power drill and .051mm metal bit
- Scissors
- Slide box: 2" silver

Instructions

1. Paint slide box red using cosmetic sponge; let dry.

2. Adhere mini playing card and crown to front of slide box with craft glue.

3. Trim photo to fit and place inside slide box. Cover inside of box with thin layer of dimensional adhesive; let dry.

4. Drill hole through one corner of each charm using C clamp, power drill, and bit. Drill hole in back of box, about 3/4" up from box bottom. Attach charms to inside of slide box with brad.

5. Drill two holes in top of box. Open one jump ring using both pliers and thread through both holes and close.

6. Attach remaining jump ring through jump ring in box top. String chain through jump ring and snap ball clasp on end.

Two Sisters

I made this necklace for my sister to wear. She has two little girls that she is very proud of and this necklace shows how adorable they are.

Materials

- Chain: medium cable (15")
- Charms: $\frac{5}{8}$" square silver (3)
- Craft glue
- Jump rings: 7mm (2); 9mm (3)
- Lobster claw clasp: 12mm silver
- Photos: $\frac{5}{8}$" square (6)
- Pliers: chain-nose, flat-nose
- Ruler
- Scissors
- Stickers: $\frac{5}{8}$" square clear pebble (6)

Instructions

1. Glue photos to front and back of square charms. Place pebble stickers on top of each photo.

2. Attach charms to chain with 9mm jump rings, spacing $1\frac{1}{2}$" between each charm, using both pliers. *Note:* It's easiest to attach a charm to the middle of the chain's length first, then measure from there to place the other two charms.

3. Attach 7mm jump rings to each end of chain using both pliers. Attach clasp to one jump ring on chain end.

time-saving tip

Double-Sided View

Adding something such as an image or patterned paper to the backside will help a piece look more polished. Charms tend to twist and turn, but if you make them double-sided, there's no need to worry about them being on backwards.

CHAPTER 4

Earrings have been around for hundreds of years and have ranged from rather simple to quite elaborate. It's time to create some unique earrings of your own. Sometimes earrings are presented with a coordinating piece like a bracelet or necklace. Consider that when you are thinking about your own memories and create two or more pieces of jewelry for one memory. Learn how to turn vintage typewriter keys, foreign currency, or bottle caps into pieces of artwork you can wear plus many other ideas. In this chapter, I will show you different ways to use charms, frames, photos, and beads to transform your recollections into keepsakes to last for years to come.

Bali Temples

I created these earrings to remind me of the time I spent in Bali when I was in college. These beautiful temples were everywhere. I took tons of photos because I wanted to remember the peaceful feeling they brought me.

Materials

- Beads: ⅛" African trading coordinating colors (4); 1" wood (2)
- Bone folder
- Color-copied images (2)
- Cosmetic sponge
- Decoupage glue
- Earring wires: 15mm silver fishhook (2)
- Head pins: 3" silver (2)
- Jump rings: 4mm silver (2)
- Nail polish remover
- Pliers: chain-nose, round-nose

Instructions

1. Transfer photocopied images onto wood beads with nail polish remover and bone folder.

2. Sponge decoupage glue on wood beads with cosmetic sponge; let dry.

3. String one wood and two African beads on head pin as shown in project photo. Bend top of head pin to form ⅛" loop using round-nose pliers. Repeat with remaining beads and head pin.

4. Connect one beaded head pin to each fishhook earring with a jump ring using both pliers.

time-saving tip

Stringing Beads

I used head pins in this project, but you could use cord or wire just as easily. When connecting earring wires to the cord or wire, refer to the double-knot tying technique in Chapter 1 to make a loop for connecting.

Coins

Whenever I travel to a foreign country I like to keep a few coins to take home. I collected these coins when I was in Canada a few years ago. I knew they would be perfect for a keepsake project.

Materials

- C clamp
- Coins: ¾" (2)
- Earring wires: 15mm silver fishhook (2)
- Jump rings: 4mm silver (4)
- Pliers: chain-nose, flat-nose
- Power drill and .070mm metal bit

Instructions

1. Drill holes in top center of each coin using C clamp, power drill, and bit.

2. Thread open jump ring through hole in each coin. Add second jump ring to each jump ring on each coin.

3. Attach jump rings to earring wires using both pliers.

time-saving tip

Drilling All at Once

When you have to drill multiple items with the same sized holes in the same spot like the coins in this project, save some time by stacking the objects on top of each other and clamping them together, then simply drill through all of the layers at once.

Denmark Tulips

When I was in Denmark I visited a park that was full of beautiful tulips. I had never seen so many tulips in one place so I took a lot of photos. Now I wear them as earrings to remind me of the colors and shapes of the flowers.

Materials

- Charms: ¾" silver frames (2)
- Dimensional adhesive
- Earring wires: 15mm silver fishhook (2)
- Photos (2)
- Pliers: chain-nose, flat-nose
- Scissors
- Tweezers

Instructions

1. Trim photos with scissors to fit frame opening and place in charms using tweezers.

2. Fill back of each frame with dimensional adhesive to add support; let dry.

3. Attach earring wires to charms using both pliers.

time-saving tip

Coordinating Photos

Some projects will use more than one photo. With this pair of earrings I chose to use images of tulips, but mixed it up by using two different colors. When you're making your own pair of earrings keep in mind that every image doesn't have to match exactly.

Hugs & Kisses

My husband found these typewriter keys at an antique store and bought them for me knowing that I love vintage stuff. I held onto the keys for awhile, not knowing what to do with them, until I realized they would make the perfect earrings.

Materials

- C clamp
- Craft glue
- Earring wires: 15mm silver fishhook (2)
- Jump rings: 7mm silver (2)
- Pliers: chain-nose, flat-nose
- Power drill and .051mm metal bit
- Vintage typewriter keys: ⅝" (2)

Instructions

1. Drill holes in backside of each type-writer key using C clamp, power drill, and bit.

2. Thread jump ring through holes in typewriter keys and attach to earring wires using both pliers.

3. Squeeze a few drops of glue where jump rings go through keys to hold rings in place; let dry.

Kennedy Kay

Kennedy is my niece who happens to live right next door. She loves to watch me create art projects while she works on her own. I made these earrings using charm frames and wooden beads to remind her of the time we spend together.

Materials

- Adhesives: craft glue, dimensional adhesive, strong-hold glue
- Beads: ⅜" wooden with initial (2)
- C clamp
- Charms: ⅞" silver oval frames (2)
- Earring posts with backs: ⅜" silver (2)
- Hemp: natural (12")
- Jump rings: 7mm silver (2)
- Photos (2)
- Pliers: chain-nose, flat-nose
- Power drill and .051mm metal bit
- Scissors

Instructions

1. Glue one photo to each frame using craft glue; let dry.

2. Trim excess photo around each frame using scissors. Cover inside of each frame with dimensional adhesive; let dry.

3. Adhere earring posts to backside of wooden beads with craft glue; let dry.

4. Drill hole in top center of each frame using C clamp, power drill, and bit. Attach jump ring to each charm frame using both pliers.

5. String hemp through wooden bead and jump ring twice and tie in a double knot. Apply a few drops of strong-hold glue to each knot to secure; let dry.

Manhattan Caps

Manhattan is one of my favorite places to visit. I decided that adding maps to bottle caps would be a great way to feature some of my favorite areas in a New York minute.

Materials

- Adhesives: craft glue, dimensional adhesive
- Bottle caps: 1¼" (2)
- C clamp
- Circle punch: 1 "

- Earring wires: 15mm silver fishhook (2)
- Map
- Pliers: chain-nose, flat-nose
- Power drill and .051mm metal bit

Instructions

1. Punch out two parts of the map with circle punch. Adhere maps to inside of bottle caps with craft glue and cover with dimensional adhesive; let dry.

2. Drill holes in top center of each bottle cap using C clamp, power drill, and bit.

3. Attach earring wires to bottle caps using both pliers.

time-saving tip

Finding a Map

If you don't have a map of an area you've visited, the Internet is a quick and easy way to find all kinds of maps. Simply add the word "images" to your search to instantly access maps from practically any area. Once you've found the one you want, click and drag it onto your computer's desktop. You can resize it or change it from color to black-and-white using photo-editing software.

Love Rules

I love the crazy photos of my husband and me in this project. Sometimes we like to just hold the camera in front of us and take a few photos. These earrings remind me of how happy and in love we are.

Materials

- Adhesives: craft glue, dimensional adhesive
- Charms: ¾" brass circle (2)
- Circle ruler
- Craft knife
- Earring wires: 15mm silver fishhook (2)
- Patterned paper scrap
- Photos (2)
- Pliers: chain-nose, flat-nose
- Stickers: ¾" round clear pebble (2)

Instructions

1. Cut two ⅝" circles from each patterned paper and photos using craft knife and circle ruler.

2. Adhere paper circles to charm fronts and photos to charm backs with craft glue; let dry.

3. Apply pebble stickers to top of paper circles. Cover photos with dimensional adhesive; let dry.

4. Attach earring wires to charms using both pliers.

time-saving tip

Embellishing Purchased Elements

Don't be afraid to add your own image or design on top of purchased charms or other products, such as ribbon slides or brads. Adhere the image to the project with craft glue and cover with dimensional adhesive or thick clear embossing powder.

Studio Inspiration

I love to go inspiration shopping for my studio. I'm always changing and adding things so I thought these two images, one of me shopping for stuff and one of the actual studio, would be perfect for earrings.

Materials

- Adhesives: craft glue, decoupage glue
- Chipboard
- Cosmetic sponge
- Earring wires: 15mm silver fishhook (2)
- Metal charm frames: 1" x ¾" silver (2)
- Patterned paper scraps: coordinating colors
- Photos (2)
- Pliers: chain-nose, flat-nose
- Ruler
- Scissors

Instructions

1. Trim each photo to fit charm frame. Cut sixteen 1" x ¾" chipboard pieces and two 1" x ¾" patterned paper pieces.

2. Layer one photo, eight pieces of chipboard, and one paper piece together with photo on one side and patterned paper on opposite side. Adhere together with craft glue. Repeat with remaining photo, chipboard pieces, and patterned paper.

3. Sponge decoupage glue on both sides of each piece using cosmetic sponge; let dry.

4. Open charm frames and insert decoupaged pieces.

5. Attach earring wires to top of metal frames using both pliers.

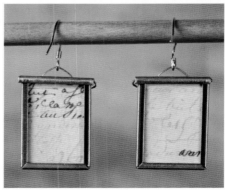

CHAPTER 5

A lapel pin is a great way to show support for someone you love or a favorite cause, or it can serve as a touching memorial to a beloved ancestor. It's also a unique way of capturing the essence of a remarkable trip. In this chapter I encourage you to spread your wings a bit and discover the multiple ways to honor loved ones and share memories. You will learn how to create photo transfers from your stash of vacation images, use charms to highlight a memory, and incorporate found objects from travels along with many other inspirational ideas. These designs can all be made into pins so you can proudly wear your heart on your sleeve, or wherever is most comfortable, for everyone to see.

Bali Experience

Visiting Bali was a remarkable experience. Everything about the island is beautiful—the people, countryside, and market places. This pin incorporates a map, coin, and photo that encompass all that I saw while I was there.

Materials

- Adhesives: craft glue, dimensional adhesive
- C clamp
- Charms: 1" x ¾", 2" x 1½" brass oval frames (1 each)
- Coin: 1" silver
- Jump rings: silver 4mm, 7mm (3)
- Map: Bali
- Photo
- Pin back: ¾" silver
- Pliers: chain-nose, flat-nose
- Power drill and .051mm metal bit
- Scissors

Instructions

1. Trim photo and map to fit oval frames. Adhere photos to frames with craft glue and cover with dimensional adhesive; let dry.

2. Drill holes in top center of small oval frame, bottom center of large oval frame, and top and bottom of coin using C clamp, power drill, and bit.

3. Connect small oval and coin together with 7mm jump ring using both pliers.

4. Connect large oval and coin together with two 7mm jump rings and 4mm jump ring, as shown in project photo.

5. Adhere pin back to center back of large oval frame with craft glue.

time-saving tip

Memorabilia Storage

After I had visited a few countries and began collecting items from my travels, I knew I'd better start keeping track of what came from where. I decided to organize my souvenirs in cigar boxes, one box per trip. If you can't find this type of box, try using cardboard or plastic shoeboxes. Make sure to label each box with the date and location of the trip.

Baseball Days

I made this pin for my sister whose sons play baseball. It's a great piece that shows her support of her boys when they are playing in a big game.

Materials

- Adhesives: craft glue, decoupage glue
- Brad: ⅛" blue
- Chipboard: 6" square
- Circle ruler
- Cosmetic sponge
- Craft knife
- Hole punch: 1/16"
- Photos: 1¼" x ¾" (3); baseball themed 1⅜"
- Pin back: ¾" silver
- Rub-ons: numbers
- Ruler

Instructions

1. Glue photos to chipboard piece using craft glue; let dry. Cut around each photo with craft knife and ruler. *Note:* Use the circle ruler and craft knife to trim around the baseball photo.

2. Adhere rub-on date to baseball photo.

3. Coat all photos with decoupage glue using cosmetic sponge; let dry.

4. Punch hole in each photo in upper left-hand corner with hole punch. Insert brad through all photos and flatten on back of baseball.

5. Glue pin back to back of baseball photo with craft glue.

time-saving tip

Pin Back Positioning

Be sure you adhere the pin back to the design correctly. I recommend putting it in the upper center of the back of the piece. Before applying the glue, check to be sure the pin opens in the right direction and isn't upside-down.

73

Beach Memories

The beach is a big part of my family's life. This pin features a photo of one of my nieces during her first summer at the beach. I thought this was a sweet way to capture her first beach experience.

Materials

- Adhesives: craft glue, dimensional adhesive
- C clamp
- Charm: ¾" brass oval frame
- Glass bottle pendant with cork: 1" x 1½"
- Jump ring: 7mm silver
- Measuring spoon
- Photo
- Pin back: ¾" silver
- Pliers: chain-nose, flat-nose
- Power drill and .051mm metal bit
- Sand
- Scissors
- Seashells: mini (6)

Instructions

1. Trim photo to fit inside oval charm with scissors. Adhere photo to oval charm with craft glue. Cover with dimensional adhesive; let dry.

2. Drill hole in bottom center of oval charm using C clamp, power drill, and bit.

3. Pour a teaspoon of sand into bottle with measuring spoon and add seashells.

4. Add a couple of drops of craft glue to cork and replace in bottle; let dry.

5. Attach bottle to oval charm with jump ring using both pliers.

6. Glue pin back to back of oval charm.

time-saving tip

Proper Pouring

When you need to pour a material like sand into a small opening such as the glass bottle in this project, make a temporary funnel out of paper. Roll a sheet of printer paper into a cone shape and insert the pointed tip into the bottle. Pour the sand into the cone, which will neatly siphon it into the bottle.

Finding Wings

My niece, Kitty, is very shy and always seems to be attached to her mother's hip. Recently, she has started to come out of her shell so I made this pin to help her mom recall when her little girl found her wings.

Materials

- Cardstock: 1½"x 1⅛" coordinating color
- Chipboard: 1½"x 1⅛"
- Craft glue
- Frame: 1½"x 1⅛" silver oval
- Metal sheet: 32-gauge silver (3½" square)
- Photo: 1½"x 1⅛"
- Pin back: ¾" silver
- Scissors
- Wings: 1½" clear plastic (2)

Instructions

1. Adhere photo, cardstock, and chipboard together in this order using craft glue; let dry.

2. Glue wings to metal sheet; let dry. Trim metal around wing edges with scissors.

3. Insert reinforced photo into frame and adhere in place using craft glue. Glue wings to frame back.

4. Adhere pin back to center back of frame; let dry.

time-saving tip

Matting Photos

Many times the photo I want to use in a jewelry project isn't the right size or shape for the frame I'm using. When that happens, I mat the photo on a piece of cardstock that either matches or coordinates with the main color in the image. Cardstock isn't strong enough to hold the weight of the pin, so the chipboard back piece is still necessary.

Mother of Peace

Knowing our ancestors is key to unlocking who we are. The peaceful look on this mother's face made me think of the love and joy she must have felt for her family then and now. The charms represent peace and security. The watch case is perfectly suited to hold tiny dimensional items such as beads, seashells, or charms. Add framed photos in place of the dangling charms for an entirely different look.

Materials

- Charms: dove, lock, mini key
- Circle punch: 1"
- Craft glue
- Craft hammer
- Jump rings: 7mm silver (3)
- Photo
- Pin back: ¾" silver
- Pliers: chain-nose, flat-nose
- Pocket watch case with glass front: 1⅜" brass

Instructions

1. Punch photo using circle punch. Glue to inside of pocket watch.

2. Close pocket watch by tapping gently on back with craft hammer.

3. Attach charms to pocket watch bezel loop with jump rings using both pliers.

4. Glue pin back to center back of pocket watch.

time-saving tip

Punch Power

Paper punches come in many shapes and sizes that make jewelry projects easier and quicker. Simply decide on the portion of the image you want to use in a project and cut it out using a paper punch. Be sure the punch's opening is centered over the image you want by flipping the punch over so you can see the opening. Position the image facing out through the opening as desired and punch as usual.

Mountain Bike Racer

My husband loves to race mountain bikes. I made this pin to wear to his races to show my support for him and all the hard work he undertakes for his passion. A simple photo change and a new charm will make it easy for you to cheer on your favorite cause.

Materials

- Adhesives: craft glue, dimensional adhesive
- Bottle cap: 1¼"
- C clamp
- Charm: silver bike
- Circle punch: 1"
- Jump rings: silver 4mm, 7mm (2)
- Photo
- Pin back: ¾" silver
- Pliers: chain-nose, flat-nose
- Power drill and .051mm metal bit

Instructions

1. Punch photo with circle punch. Adhere inside bottle cap with craft glue; let dry. Cover image with dimensional adhesive; let dry.

2. Drill hole in bottom center of bottle cap using C clamp, power drill, and bit.

3. Link jump rings and attach charm to bottle cap as shown in project photo using both pliers.

4. Glue pin back to center back of bottle cap with craft glue; let dry.

time-saving tip

Charming Charms

Charms are available in an enormous variety of styles. Many companies make them for all types of hobbies and interests. When you think of charms, you may think of something feminine, but don't be afraid to look beyond what is normal or expected. The bike charm used in this project was the perfect complement to the photo.

Photo Search

This piece is about me. I'm always looking for a new direction and ideas with my photography. The photo I used shows me with my camera around my neck like it is on most trips. The ornate frame in this project would work well for an ancestral portrait. Choosing a different style of frame will add a whole new dimension to the piece.

Materials

- Adhesives: craft glue, decoupage glue
- Bone folder
- C clamp
- Charm: $\frac{5}{8}$" brass compass
- Chipboard: 3"x 2"
- Color-copied image
- Cosmetic sponge
- Craft knife
- Frame: 3"x 2" brass
- Jump ring: 7mm silver
- Nail polish remover
- Patterned paper scrap: coordinating color
- Pin back: $\frac{3}{4}$" silver
- Pliers: chain-nose, flat-nose
- Power drill and .051mm metal bit

Instructions

1. Transfer photocopied image onto patterned paper with nail polish remover and bone folder.

2. Adhere transferred image to chipboard and coat with decoupage glue using cosmetic sponge; let dry. *Note:* This will support the image and protect it from scratches.

3. Glue chipboard piece to back of frame with image showing through front. Trim excess chipboard with craft knife as needed.

4. Drill hole in bottom right corner of frame using C clamp, power drill, and bit, as shown in project photo.

5. Connect charm and frame with jump ring using both pliers.

6. Attach pin back to back of chipboard with craft glue; let dry.

Time to Eat

I enjoy being in the kitchen at my mom's house. I cherish the time and the love she puts into our family meals. Many of my favorite memories involve the entire family sitting down to enjoy dinner together on Sunday evening. A clock is a great way to call to mind an occasion that happened at a particular time. You could create a pin featuring the time of your family's game night and a favorite game you play.

Materials

- Bottle cap: 1"
- Brad: ⅛" blue
- C clamp
- Clock: 1" chipboard
- Clock hands: 3" brass
- Craft glue
- Fork: 2½" brass
- Jump ring: 7mm silver
- Pin back: ¾" silver
- Pliers: chain-nose, flat-nose
- Power drill and .051mm metal bit

Instructions

1. Adhere clock to inside of bottle cap with craft glue; let dry.

2. Drill hole in center of clock and below the number 5 using C clamp, power drill, and bit. Attach clock hands to clock through center hole using brad.

3. Attach fork to bottle cap with jump ring using both pliers.

4. Glue pin back to back of bottle cap; let dry.

time-saving tip

Tool Time

One tool that seems to be the handiest when making memory jewelry is a power drill and metal cutting bits. A cordless drill isn't necessary, but it's easy to work with because the length of the cord doesn't limit you and it doesn't get in the way as you work. Keep a scrap piece of wood handy to work on so you don't accidentally bore into your work surface.

CHAPTER 6

I think lockets are very special pieces of jewelry. Lockets hold secrets and memories, and are filled with love. I find them very intriguing and whenever I see someone wearing one I always wonder what's inside. When I was a little girl my mother gave me a locket that held a picture of my dad and her. She told me that I should always wear it to remember how much they love me. The lockets in this chapter can be worn around your neck, used as a key chain, or hung on your shirt as a pin. Some lockets can even be made as a mini scrapbook to hold precious photos. Lockets have so many possibilities, so come explore some of them in the following pages.

Cowgirl

I made this locket for my niece. One year she had the opportunity to dress up like a real cowgirl and ride a horse and pet a buffalo. She'll always treasure that day and this special locket will let her share those memories with friends.

Materials

- Adhesives: craft glue, decoupage glue
- Brads: ⅛" green (4)
- Chain: silver small cable (16")
- Charm: silver horseshoe
- Cosmetic sponge
- Dog tags: 2" x 1⅛" brass (2)
- Hole punch: ⅛"
- Jump rings: 7mm silver (4)
- Lobster claw clasp: 12mm
- Metal hinge: ¾" brass
- Patterned paper scraps: coordinating colors
- Photos: 1¼" x 1" (2)
- Pliers: chain-nose, flat-nose
- Sandpaper
- Scissors

Instructions

1. Glue patterned paper to both sides of dog tags using craft glue. Trim excess patterned paper.

2. Sand all edges of tags using sandpaper.

3. Trim both photos to fit inside tags and adhere with craft glue; let dry. Coat both sides of tags with decoupage glue using cosmetic sponge; let dry.

4. Stack tags with photos facing each other. Punch one hole in top center and two holes on left edge of tags. Attach tags together with hinge and brads.

5. Attach charm to front dog tag through top hole with jump ring using both pliers.

6. Attach a second jump ring to back tag through top hole and thread chain through ring. Add third jump ring to one end of chain and clasp to other end using remaining jump ring. *Note:* Hook clasp to both jump rings attached to top of locket to hold it closed when wearing.

Dayton Family

I made this key chain for my sister. It holds several photos of her and her family at one of their favorite places to visit, the beach.

Materials

- Adhesives: craft glue, decoupage glue
- Ball chain with clasp: silver (3")
- Button: ½" round with sailboat picture
- C clamp
- Cosmetic sponge
- Head pin: silver 3"
- Jump rings: 9mm silver (2)
- Metal squares: 1½" brown monogram (2)
- Patterned papers: coordinating colors
- Photos: 1¼" x ⅞" (9)
- Pliers: chain-nose, flat-nose, round-nose
- Power drill and .051mm metal bit

Instructions

1. Cut eighteen 1½" squares of patterned paper and adhere back to back with pattern facing out using craft glue, creating nine square pages; let dry.

2. Glue photos to each side of paper pages; let dry.

3. Coat both sides of all pages using decoupage glue and cosmetic sponge; let dry.

4. Stack pages between metal squares and drill holes ⅜" from left and right edges through entire stack using C clamp, power drill, and bit. Drill one hole in back of metal square ⅜" from bottom right corner edge. Secure stack together with jump rings using two of the pliers.

5. Insert head pin through hole in back metal square. Thread button onto head pin and wrap wire twice around itself to secure using Head Pin Wrapping technique in Chapter 1.

6. Thread chain through jump rings and snap clasp closed.

Friendship

This project features photos of a good friend of mine who happens to live in Australia. I was lucky enough to visit her in her hometown one year.

Materials

- Adhesives: craft glue, decoupage glue, dimensional adhesive
- Chain: silver medium wide cable (18")
- Chipboard: 1⅛" circles (4)
- Circle box with clear top: 1¼" silver
- Cosmetic sponge
- Jump rings: silver 7mm, 9mm (1 each)
- Patterned paper: coordinating colors
- Photos: 1⅛" circle (4)
- Piercing tool
- Pliers: chain-nose, flat-nose
- Rub-ons: numbers
- Sandpaper
- Sewing needle
- Thread: pink
- Toggle clasp: medium silver

Instructions

1. Cut four 1⅛" circles from patterned papers. Glue photo and circle to each side of chipboard circles using craft glue; let dry. Sand around edges of photos and patterned paper with sandpaper.

2. Coat both sides of embellished circles with decoupage glue and cosmetic sponge; let dry.

3. Stack embellished circles and pierce hole in top center of stack. Thread needle and insert through stack. Tie in ½" loop using a double knot.

4. Adhere one jump ring to top back of box to protrude halfway above edge using dimensional adhesive; let dry.

5. Apply rub-on numbers to box lid and coat with decoupage glue; let dry. Thread chain through jump ring. Attach clasp to ends with jump rings using both pliers.

Full Heart

I cherish the photos of my husband and me. This is a wonderful way to hold these photos close to my heart.

Materials

- Acrylic paint: red
- C clamp
- Chipboard: 6" squares
- Cloth
- Craft glue
- Jump rings: 9mm silver (2)
- Key ring: silver
- Metal hearts: 1½" ornate silver (2)
- Patterned paper scraps: coordinating colors
- Pencil
- Photos (4)
- Pliers: chain-nose, flat-nose
- Power drill and .070mm metal bit
- Scissors

Instructions

1. Trace metal heart onto chipboard, patterned paper, and photos; cut out all heart shapes.

2. Adhere one chipboard heart to backside of each metal heart; let dry. Glue one paper heart to backside of each metal heart, sandwiching chipboard in the middle.

3. Glue photos to front of remaining chipboard hearts and patterned paper to back.

4. Rub paint on front of both metal hearts with cloth. Wipe off excess, allowing embossed design to show; let dry.

5. Stack all hearts together with metal hearts facing out on front and back. Drill holes in left side of stack as shown in project photo using C clamp, power drill, and bit.

6. Thread rings through holes in hearts and close using both pliers. Attach pre-made key ring to top jump ring.

Graduation Day

The seventh and last child to graduate from high school is quite an accomplishment for a parent. I made this pin locket for my mother-in-law. She did an amazing job raising her children and this was one of her proudest moments.

Materials

- Adhesives: craft glue, dimensional adhesive
- Brad: ½" copper fleur-de-lis
- Chipboard: ¼" numbers (4)
- Circle ruler
- Craft knife
- Matchbox: 2"x 1¼"x ½" white
- Patterned papers: coordinating colors (2)
- Photos (6)
- Piercing tool
- Pin back: ¾" silver
- Ruler
- Scissors
- Stickers: alphabet, label tab
- Ticket stub: 2"x 1" pink
- Typewriter key: ½" copper

Instructions

1. Trim photo to fit inside typewriter key with circle ruler and craft knife.

2. Adhere photo inside key with craft glue; let dry. Cover image with dimensional adhesive; let dry.

3. Cut one 7"x 2" patterned paper strip with scissors. Glue around matchbox sleeve using craft glue; let dry.

4. Adhere ticket stub, chipboard numbers, and typewriter key to matchbox sleeve lid. Add alphabet sticker as desired.

5. Pierce hole in top of lid and insert brad, flattening prongs on backside.

6. Cut one 1¼"x 12" coordinating patterned paper strip. Trim five photos to 1¾"x 1¼" and glue to paper strip, leaving ⅛" gap between each photo.

7. Accordion-fold photo strip and adhere left end of strip to inside bottom of box.

8. Add label tab to right end of photo strip and embellish as desired.

9. Glue pin back to matchbox lid back; let dry.

Matchbox Memories

So many memories can be held in a matchbox. I made this pin locket to hold photos of visiting Amsterdam. I never want to forget seeing that historic city for the first time.

Materials

- Adhesives: craft glue, decoupage glue
- Charm: brass heart with wings
- Cosmetic sponge
- Hole punch: $\frac{1}{16}$"
- Jump ring: 7mm silver
- Map: Amsterdam
- Matchbox: 2"x 1½"x ½" white
- Metal corner: 1" ornate brass
- Patterned paper scraps: coordinating colors (5)
- Photos (5)
- Pin back: ¾" silver
- Pliers: chain-nose, flat-nose
- Ruler
- Scissors
- Train ticket stub

Instructions

1. Cut one 2"x 6" and one 2"x 1½" piece of map. Wrap 2"x 6" piece around matchbox sleeve and adhere using decoupage glue and cosmetic sponge; let dry. Trim excess paper.

2. Glue ticket stub and brass corner to lid and remaining map piece to inside bottom of box with craft glue; let dry.

3. Trim photos and five pieces of patterned paper to 1¾"x 1¼".

4. Glue one photo and one paper piece together, back to back. Repeat with remaining photos and paper pieces; let dry.

5. Coat both sides of all photo pieces with decoupage glue; let dry.

6. Stack photos and punch hole in top left corner.

7. Thread open jump ring through stack and charm; close using both pliers.

8. Place mini-book inside matchbox and slide cover over box. Adhere pin back on sleeve back using craft glue; let dry.

60th Birthday

My mom threw a surprise party for my dad's 60th birthday. It was quite a night with all of us together as a family to help him celebrate. I created a locket that can be a key chain or a necklace in honor of the occasion.

Materials

- Acrylic paint: black
- Adhesives: craft glue, dimensional adhesive
- Bead: 1/8" African
- C clamp
- Chain: silver small cable (18")
- Cloth
- Embossing stylus
- Head pin: 3" silver
- Inkpad: black
- Jump rings: 7mm silver (4)
- Metal sheets: 1 1/2" x 1 1/4" 32-gauge silver nickel (2)
- Photos: 1 1/8" x 1 3/8" (2)
- Pliers: chain-nose, flat-nose
- Power drill and .051mm metal bit
- Rubber stamps: numbers
- Scissors
- Toggle clasp: medium silver
- Wire: 20-gauge black cloth-covered (3")
- Wire cutters

Instructions

1. Emboss designs on metal sheets using rubber stamps, embossing stylus, and acrylic paint.

2. Trim photos to fit inside metal sheets using scissors. Adhere photos to sheets and cover with dimensional adhesive; let dry.

time-saving tip

Folding Metal
Metal sheets are easy to work with because they are so thin and can be cut with scissors or a hole punch. Cut metal has a sharp edge on it but you can bend the edges over to conceal the dangerous sides. Decide how far down you want to bend the metal and mark a line with a pencil and ruler. Begin folding the edge over using flat-nose pliers until it is far enough over to flatten with your fingers.

Top: The inside of the locket contains favorite photos of the occasion. **Above:** The bead on the back of the locket provides a secure place to wrap a wire closure around, holding the locket closed.

3. Drill two holes on left side edge of sheets, $\frac{1}{2}$" from top and bottom, using C clamp, power drill, and bit. Drill second hole through both sheets on middle right-side edge. Stack sheets so holes are aligned.

4. Attach two jump rings through holes on left side using both pliers.

5. String bead onto head pin and thread through right-side hole in bottom metal sheet. Cut head pin with wire cutters so it extends $\frac{1}{16}$" beyond hole. Using dimensional adhesive, secure pin in place; let dry. Flip locket over and apply dimensional adhesive on and around bead and head of pin; let dry.

6. Fold wire in half and thread ends through right-side hole on top metal sheet, bending ends up around edge. Add a few drops of dimensional adhesive to wire ends to secure; let dry.

7. Bend wire loop around edge and fold to backside of locket, wrapping around bead.

8. String chain through top left jump ring and attach clasp with remaining jump rings.

time-saving tip
Take More Photos

Every time I return from a vacation, traveling, or a special event, I always wish I had taken more photos. For instance, I ended up having very few photos from my dad's birthday. I was so sad when I got home and looked through my snapshots. If you are taking photos with a digital camera, you are only limited by the size of your memory card. It's always better to have more photos of an occasion than not enough, so snap away!

Snowboarding

At 8 years old, my niece is already a good snowboarder. I made this for her gear bag as a reminder of the fun times on the slopes.

Materials

- Adhesives: craft glue, decoupage glue
- Ball chain and clasp: silver (3")
- Chipboard shapes: $1\frac{3}{4}$" circles (5)
- Cosmetic sponge
- Hole punch: $\frac{1}{8}$"
- Map: ski run
- Patterned paper scraps: blue lines, red snowflake
- Photos: $1\frac{3}{4}$" x $1\frac{3}{8}$" (4)
- Rub-ons: alphabet, numbers
- Ruler
- Sandpaper
- Scissors

Instructions

1. Adhere blue patterned paper to one side of each of the four chipboard circles and red snowflake paper to one side of remaining circle with craft glue; let dry.

2. Cut map into $1\frac{3}{4}$" squares and glue to backsides of all circles; let dry. Trim excess paper. Sand around edges of all circles as desired.

3. Adhere photos on top of blue line-covered circles and trim excess.

4. Rub letter and number on red snowflake-covered circle as desired.

5. Coat both sides of all chipboard circles with decoupage glue and cosmetic sponge; let dry.

6. Stack circles and punch hole in top left corner with hole punch. Thread chain through holes and snap clasp closed.

time-saving tip

Carry It With You

Carry a disposable camera when you're traveling. It's easier to take on a vigorous activity that could potentially damage more expensive equipment. If you want to use the images from a film camera on your computer, just request that the photos also be put on a CD when you have the film developed.

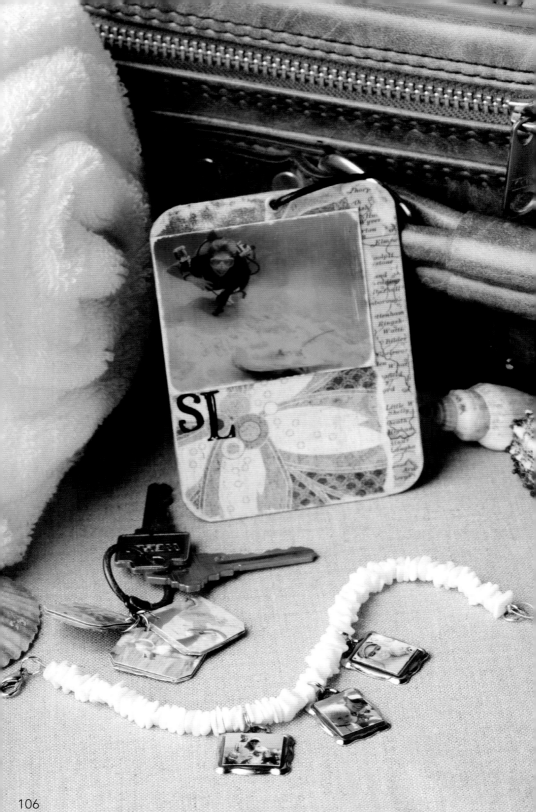

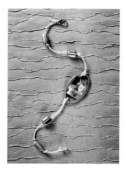

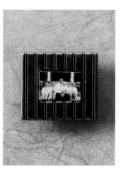

CHAPTER 7

The possibilities are nearly endless when it comes to jewelry accessories. When thinking about what makes an accessory, consider barrettes to wear in your hair, key rings to carry keys and hold memories, tags to adorn luggage or purses, or a sentimental tie tac made just for your husband's tie. In the following pages I explore several different items that can be worn or carried to remind you of the vacations you've taken, good times with your family, and adventures you've had. The projects in this chapter will open your eyes to the potential of different pieces of jewelry that you don't normally see worn every day but really could be, especially when it is a keepsake piece that holds a dear memory.

Accessories

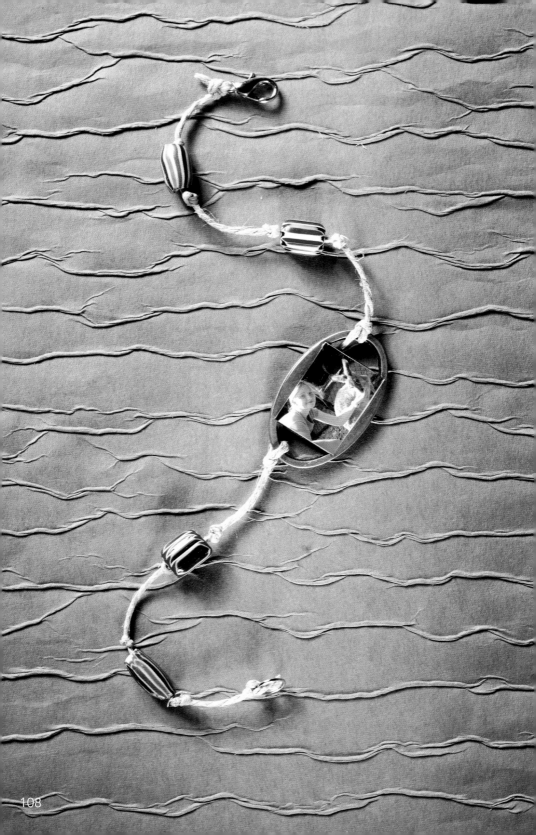

Australian Anklet

My niece, Sierra, and her family went to Australia one year on vacation. They got to do so many fun things and explore new parts of the world. I made this anklet for her with a photo from her trip.

Materials

- Adhesives: craft glue, dimensional adhesive
- Beads: ½" African (4)
- Hemp: natural (12")
- Jump ring: 7mm silver
- Lobster claw clasp: 12mm silver
- Photo: ⅞" x ¾"
- Ribbon slide: 1½" silver

Instructions

1. Adhere photo to ribbon slide with craft glue; let dry. Cover with dimensional adhesive; let dry.

2. String one bead onto hemp 2" from one end of strand. Tie a single knot on either side of bead to secure in place.

3. String second bead onto hemp 1" from previous bead and tie knots as in Step 2.

4. String ribbon slide onto hemp 1" from second bead and tie single knot around one side of the ribbon slide. Weave hemp under ribbon slide and tie another single knot on opposite side.

5. String third bead onto hemp 1" from ribbon slide and tie knots as in Step 2. Repeat for final bead.

6. Thread clasp onto hemp 1" from final bead and tie in a double knot.

7. Attach jump ring to opposite end of hemp, 1" from bead, and tie in a double knot.

time-saving tip

Make It Your Own

Any project can be altered to fit your memory. You could make this same type of anklet with an entirely different feel by simply changing the style of beads and stringing material. Crystal beads and narrow satin ribbon suggest a more feminine feel while shells and rustic beads imply a beach theme.

Beach Anklet

My sister has a family of five boys including her husband. I made this anklet with photos of her family at the beach.

Materials

- Adhesives: craft glue, dimensional adhesive
- Beads: ¼" white puka shells (approx. 80)
- Charms: ¾" silver frame (3)
- Crimp beads: silver (2)
- Jump rings: 7mm silver (3)
- Lobster claw clasp: 12mm silver
- Photos (3)
- Pliers: chain-nose, flat-nose
- Scissors
- Wire: 26-gauge silver (12")

Instructions

1. Trim photos to fit inside each charm using scissors. Adhere inside charms with craft glue.

2. Cover each photo with dimensional adhesive; let dry.

3. Thread wire through crimp bead and make a small loop about ½". Thread wire end back through crimp bead and flatten using chain-nose pliers.

4. String beads on 2½" length of wire. Add first charm and string beads on 1" of wire. Repeat with remaining charms, filling remaining wire length after final charm with beads. Finish with remaining crimp bead.

5. Attach one jump ring to each looped end using both pliers.

6. Attach clasp to jump ring on one end of anklet and final jump ring to ring on opposite end.

time-saving tip

Trading Out Photos
If you don't have photos of the memory you want to capture, swap out the photos that would have been used in the project for other items such as seashells, charms, a game piece, or coins with holes drilled in them.

Beach Key Ring

I made this key chain with a wave-like design for my parents' beach house. They can keep their house key on it as a reminder of all the summers our family has spent with them at the beach.

Materials

- Acrylic paints: black, blue
- Adhesives: craft glue, dimensional adhesive
- Book ring: 1" silver
- Cosmetic sponge
- Embossing stylus
- Hole punch: 1/16"
- Inkpad: permanent black
- Jump rings: 7mm silver (3)
- Metal sheets: 1" x 3/4" 32-gauge silver (3)
- Photos (3)
- Pliers: chain-nose, flat-nose
- Rubber stamp: wave
- Ruler
- Scissors

Instructions

1. Emboss designs on metal sheet using rubber stamp, inkpad, and embossing stylus.

2. Paint black and blue on waves using cosmetic sponge to highlight areas of waves; let dry.

3. Fold sides of embossed pieces over 1/8" using pliers to create a blunt, straight edge.

4. Trim photos to fit back of each silver piece with scissors and adhere with craft glue; let dry. Cover images with dimensional adhesive; let dry.

5. Punch hole in same corner of each wave piece with hole punch.

6. Attach jump ring to each silver piece using both pliers. Thread jump rings onto book ring.

Dad's Key Ring

This key ring features photos of my brother-in-law and his kids on a dirt bike outing. It will remind him of a good day spent with his kids.

Materials

- Adhesives: craft glue, dimensional adhesive
- Bottle caps: 1¼" (3)
- C clamp
- Circle punch: 1"
- Cosmetic sponge
- Embossing ink
- Embossing powder: matte brown
- Heat tool
- Jump rings: 7mm silver (3)
- Photos (3)
- Pliers: chain-nose, flat-nose
- Power drill and .051mm metal bit
- Split ring: ¾" silver

Instructions

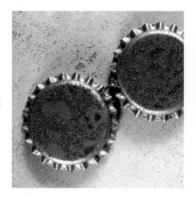

1. Dab embossing ink on backside of all bottle caps using cosmetic sponge. Shake embossing powder over top of embossing ink and tap off excess. Heat powder with heat tool until melted; let cool.

2. Cut out photos with circle punch and adhere inside each bottle cap. Cover photos with dimensional adhesive; let dry.

3. Drill holes in top center of one bottle cap and top and bottom center of remaining bottle caps using C clamp, power drill, and bit.

4. Link bottle caps together using jump rings and both pliers as shown in project photo. Attach split ring to top bottle cap with remaining jump ring.

time-saving tip

Adding Realistic Embellishments

In this project I wanted to give the appearance of dirt, so I used brown embossing powder. Options for other projects might be adding ultra-fine glitter to a flower to suggest sunshine or acrylic jewels on a crown for a regal appearance.

Dive Luggage Tag

My sister and her husband love to go diving and have done so all over the world. This is the perfect gift for her to add to her dive bag to represent all of the great diving trips they have gone on together.

Materials

- Adhesives: craft glue, decoupage glue
- Chipboard: 3"x 4"
- Cord: black leather (12")
- Corner rounder
- Cosmetic sponge
- Eyelet: ⅛" blue
- Eyelet setting tools
- Hole punch: ⅛"
- Patterned papers: coordinating colors (2–3)
- Photo: 2"x 3"
- Rub-ons: alphabet

Instructions

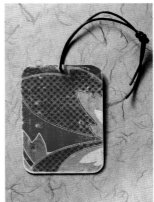

1. Cover chipboard with patterned papers as desired using craft glue; let dry.

2. Shape corners of tag with corner rounder.

3. Adhere photo to front of tag. Add rub-ons as desired.

4. Coat front and back of tag with decoupage glue and cosmetic sponge; let dry.

5. Punch hole in top center of tag with ⅛" hole punch; set eyelet.

6. Loop cord and thread through eyelet and tie single knot at end of cord.

time-saving tip

Protecting Your Project

Adding a layer of decoupage over the top of your project will protect it from wear and tear. This is especially helpful when using a photo on the surface of a project. The decoupage glue will protect the photo from fingerprints and smudges.

Family Love Barrette

I made this barrette for my niece, Rivers, to showcase her family. Just think how fun it will be for her to wear this to school to show and tell about how much she loves them.

Materials

- Barrette with oval stone: 2½" silver
- Charm: silver heart
- Dimensional adhesive
- Heat tool
- Jump rings: 4mm silver (2)
- Pencil
- Photo
- Pliers: chain-nose, flat-nose
- Scissors
- Screwdriver: flat-head

Instructions

1. Heat barrette stone with heat tool and pop stone out with screwdriver.

2. Trace around photo using stone as a guide. Cut out photo and adhere to inside of barrette oval with dimensional adhesive; let dry.

3. Fill oval frame with dimensional adhesive; let dry.

4. Link jump rings and charm using both pliers and attach to barrette.

time-saving tip

Add Your Own Touch

There are many different types of barrettes and most of them can easily be transformed into a keepsake hair accessory. If you find a barrette that doesn't already have a base attached to it, don't worry. You can always use craft glue or dimensional adhesive to add your own frame, button, or charm.

Four Boys Tie Tac

I made this tie tac for my brother-in-law. This photo was taken on Easter Sunday and I thought it would be a neat idea to make one each year for him so he would have a collection featuring his boys growing up.

Materials

- Adhesives: craft glue, dimensional adhesive
- Charm: 1" silver square frame
- Photo
- Scissors
- Tie tac: ½" silver

Instructions

1. Trim photo to fit inside metal frame.

2. Adhere photo to inside of frame with craft glue. Cover front of image with dimensional adhesive; let dry.

3. Glue tie tac to back center.

time-saving tip

Adapting to All Occasions

This project could easily be changed to fit any occasion, such as a wedding or other special event. The tie tac would be a simple gift to give each of the groomsmen. Personalize a tie tac with an image of the groom and his friends in the wedding party.

Music Memories Barrette

My niece, Elle, plays the piano and participates in recitals. I thought this would be a great barrette for her to wear to her performances.

Materials

- Adhesives: craft glue, decoupage glue, dimensional adhesive
- Barrette: 2½" brass
- Button: 1¼" clear
- Charm: ¾" silver frame
- Cosmetic sponge
- Craft knife
- Jump ring: 7mm silver
- Patterned paper scrap: music-themed
- Photo
- Pliers: chain-nose, flat-nose
- Power drill and .051mm metal bit
- Rub-ons: key, numbers
- Scissors

Instructions

1. Adhere patterned paper to backside of button with decoupage glue; let dry.

2. Trim excess patterned paper from around button with craft knife. Add rub-ons to top of button.

3. Coat top of button using decoupage glue and cosmetic sponge; let dry.

4. Drill hole in bottom right area of button with drill and bit. Trim photo to fit inside charm with scissors. Cover image with dimensional adhesive; let dry.

5. Attach charm and button together with jump ring using both pliers.

6. Attach barrette to back of button with craft glue; let dry.

Gallery of Decorative Paper

Sometimes finding just the right decorative paper can take more than minutes, so we've provided a sampling of some of our favorites on the following pages. Simply color copy the page and incorporate in any of the projects featured throughout this book.

Gallery of Decorative Paper

Gallery of Decorative Paper

About the Author

Liz Eaton has always had a passion for arts and crafts. Ever since she was little she dreamed of being an artist who could make art all day and not have a worry in the world.

Liz was born and raised in Phoenix, Arizona. She is the baby of a family of six kids who have all dipped their hands in artistic endeavors at some point in their lives. Her grandmother was an extreme craftswoman and was always sewing or painting. Liz has taken after her grandmother and spends her days creating in her studio. Her obsession with jewelry started in high school and grew when she decided to major in metal arts/jewelry making. Shortly after earning her bachelor's degree from Arizona State University Liz discovered the world of scrapbooking and paper crafting. She worked as a product designer for a scrapbooking company for two years and during that time she decided that teaching scrapbooking and paper crafting was her true passion. Liz now owns and runs TheAnyWhereStudio.com website offering online and kit classes that teach paper crafting techniques. She shares the beauty of making jewelry combined with paper crafting to create amazing, wearable works of art.

Liz lives in Phoenix with her husband, David, and their newborn son.

Special Thanks

I have to thank my husband for being my biggest supporter, for staying up late with me in my studio while I work. I couldn't have finished this book without his support, encouragement, and patience. I also need to thank my mom and sisters for all the photos of them and their families. I wouldn't have half as many memories if it weren't for them and all the good times we get to spend together as a family. I am so grateful for the closeness I share with my family and look forward to making more memories with them in the years to come.

METRIC EQUIVALENCY CHARTS

inches to millimeters and centimeters
(mm-millimeters, cm-centimeters)

inches	mm	cm	inches	cm	inches	cm
⅛	3	0.3	9	22.9	30	76.2
¼	6	0.6	10	25.4	31	78.7
½	13	1.3	12	30.5	33	83.8
⅝	16	1.6	13	33.0	34	86.4
¾	19	1.9	14	35.6	35	88.9
⅞	22	2.2	15	38.1	36	91.4
1	25	2.5	16	40.6	37	94.0
1¼	32	3.2	17	43.2	38	96.5
1½	38	3.8	18	45.7	39	99.1
1¾	44	4.4	19	48.3	40	101.6
2	51	5.1	20	50.8	41	104.1
2½	64	6.4	21	53.3	42	106.7
3	76	7.6	22	55.9	43	109.2
3½	89	8.9	23	58.4	44	111.8
4	102	10.2	24	61.0	45	114.3
4½	114	11.4	25	63.5	46	116.8
5	127	12.7	26	66.0	47	119.4
6	152	15.2	27	68.6	48	121.9
7	178	17.8	28	71.1	49	124.5
8	203	20.3	29	73.7	50	127.0

yards to meters

yards	meters	yards	meters	yards	meters	yards	meters	yards	meters
⅛	0.11	2⅛	1.94	4⅛	3.77	6⅛	5.60	8⅛	7.43
¼	0.23	2¼	2.06	4¼	3.89	6¼	5.72	8¼	7.54
⅜	0.34	2⅜	2.17	4⅜	4.00	6⅜	5.83	8⅜	7.66
½	0.46	2½	2.29	4½	4.11	6½	5.94	8½	7.77
⅝	0.57	2⅝	2.40	4⅝	4.23	6⅝	6.06	8⅝	7.89
¾	0.69	2¾	2.51	4¾	4.34	6¾	6.17	8¾	8.00
⅞	0.80	2⅞	2.63	4⅞	4.46	6⅞	6.29	8⅞	8.12
1	0.91	3	2.74	5	4.57	7	6.40	9	8.23
1⅛	1.03	3⅛	2.86	5⅛	4.69	7⅛	6.52	9⅛	8.34
1¼	1.14	3¼	2.97	5¼	4.80	7¼	6.63	9¼	8.46
1⅜	1.26	3⅜	3.09	5⅜	4.91	7⅜	6.74	9⅜	8.57
1½	1.37	3½	3.20	5½	5.03	7½	6.86	9½	8.69
1⅝	1.49	3⅝	3.31	5⅝	5.14	7⅝	6.97	9⅝	8.80
1¾	1.60	3¾	3.43	5¾	5.26	7¾	7.09	9¾	8.92
1⅞	1.71	3⅞	3.54	5⅞	5.37	7⅞	7.20	9⅞	9.03
2	1.83	4	3.66	6	5.49	8	7.32	10	9.14

INDEX